WORK LIFE

A Survival Guide to the Modern Office

DOVETAIL

WORK LIFE

A Survival Guide to the Modern Office

By Molly Erman

Illustrations by Chris Santone

D

DOVETAIL

TABLE OF CONTENTS

INTRODUCTION (6)

CHAPTER 1: GET ORGANIZED (8)

CHAPTER 2: EXPRESS YOURSELF (22)

CHAPTER 3: FOOD, SNACKS, AND THE OFFICE KITCHEN (36)

CHAPTER 4: KEEP IT HEALTHY (48)

CHAPTER 5: OFFICE CULTURE (70)

CHAPTER 6: WORK RELATIONSHIPS (90)

CHAPTER 7: STAYING COOL AND SAVING FACE (104)

CHAPTER 8: THE BOSS (118)

CHAPTER 9: MEETINGS (130)

CHAPTER 10: OUT OF THE OFFICE:
VACATIONS AND SICK DAYS (140)

CHAPTER 11: THE TOUGH STUFF (154)

CHAPTER 12: MOVING ON UP (164)

CHAPTER 13: THE EXIT (174)

INTRODUCTION

Just before starting my first postcollege job at a magazine in New York City, I spent nearly a summer's worth of tips I'd earned working at a bar (it should have been more, but I was a terrible bartender) on a navy blue suit. In my eyes, it represented total professionalism, and I justified its cost knowing that I would wear it for years—maybe even forever. It's a decade later now, and I'm the director of communications for a company in Brooklyn. I occasionally (okay, frequently) wear ripped jeans to work, and I have no idea where that suit is.

The meaning of "the office" has changed. Today, having an actual office, complete with a door that actually closes, is a rarity. For example, I work in a former warehouse where I don't have a landline phone and my workspace is basically anywhere I plant myself. Our elders likely did not anticipate the routine presence of a Ping-Pong table, "office dogs," or beer on tap at work. Sometimes the office is a converted loft or a snug corner in a coffee shop. And sometimes the office requires a navy blue suit—or a few of them.

Although the modern workplace has evolved, one thing that has remained unchanged is the value of doing good work, the definition of which, unlike that of the dress code, prevails across all industries. What "good work" means is being trustworthy, organized, proud of what you do, and willing to pitch in when a little extra is needed. (Of course, thriving in the workplace involves a lot more than that, which is why this book is more than one page long.)

I don't work in HR. I'm neither a recruiter nor a guidance counselor. Instead, I'm someone who spent the whole of my twenties trying to figure out the meaning of "good work." I've been lucky to have worked with incredibly intelligent, successful people, and I've learned a lot from them—and from trying to keep up with them.

This book is filled with the advice that I could have used right around the time I bought that suit. It will help you get—and stay—organized and fight through the distractions that can derail your day. There are tips on how to write productive emails, avoid snafus on social media, and turn down office mooches who try to dump their work in your lap. Curious how to fake an illness, ask for time off, or request a raise? That's all here, too, along with strategic advice for dating a coworker, breaking up (and crying discreetly) at work, freelancing without jeopardizing your day job, staring at your computer without going blind, and more.

I've been given lots of professional-career advice over the years, but my favorite piece comes from my grandfather, who told me always to "walk in like you own the place." In other words, enter with a relaxed yet obvious confidence (and perhaps a little swagger, too). It is advice that I have followed—with varying degrees of success—on every first day of school straight through college. In my adult life, I return to it anytime I'm stepping into a situation that makes me feel uneasy. My hope is that this book will help you feel like you own the place—whatever that place may look like. (And I hope that someday you really do own it.)

—MOLLY ERMAN

GET ORGANIZED

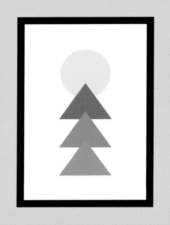

PERSONALIZE YOUR SPACE

Some companies embrace their employees' desires to add personal touches to their workspace. Others, not so much. Here are a few ideas on how to give your office, cubicle (or whatever) some personality, even if you can't get away with displaying your entire taxidermy collection:

● Hang some art, such as maps, not-too-personal photos, and colorful abstract images.

● Buy a hardy plant, like a small, sturdy succulent or a no-fuss cactus.

● Install a small desk lamp to add a studious vibe and soften harsh overhead lighting.

● Curate a modest library that covers both your professional and personal interests, and use interesting objects—a piece of quartz, an antique paperweight—for bookends.

● Mix in a statement piece, whether it's a desktop sculpture or a souvenir from a favorite trip.

KEEP A NO-MESS DESK

It's hard to feel relaxed (and productive) in a messy home. The same goes for your workspace. Excess paper, dirty take-out containers, and other refuse can create a foundational layer of unnecessary clutter. Don't let them! At the end of each day, ruthlessly toss out (or file away) anything you won't need the next morning. This evening cleansing ritual is a satisfying close to the workday and provides a refreshing head start on a productive morning.

ORGANIZE YOUR INBOX

Keeping the fury of your inbox down to a dull roar—or, more ambitiously, a whimper—requires commitment. Few things will make you more crazy than seeing "4,000 unread messages" hovering above your mail icon. You don't have to shoot for Inbox Zero, but you should at least aim for Inbox Under Control.

TACKLE THE EXISTING SITUATION:

● Delete all old emails that relate to completed projects.

● Aggressively unsubscribe from all unwanted newsletters.

● Create categorized email folders, then file correspondence accordingly.

MANAGE INCOMING EMAILS LIKE A PRO:

● Delete newsletters and nonurgent emails as soon as you've read them.

● Avoid starting a new email chain if a corresponding chain has already been established.

● Once a task or issue has been resolved, delete the chain of conversation.

● With priority mail squared away in designated folders, schedule daily sweeps of your inbox to keep it tidy.

PRIORITIZE DAILY TASKS

The first thing Monday morning, take stock of the week ahead. Make a list of your most pressing tasks and include a realistic snapshot of the work required to complete each of them. Focus on the most time-sensitive and time-consuming projects, then set blocks of time on your calendar to tackle each of them. By prescheduling to-dos as if they're meetings, you have streamlined a plan of attack that will help you stay on task.

GET GOOD AT THE SMALL STUFF

You're usually going to be your own best assistant, today and throughout your career. Take the time now to master the small-but-important details—such as calendar scheduling, submitting expenses, booking travel, or ordering supplies—because those foundational tasks never go away.

FIGHT DISTRACTIONS

At any given time, many things are fighting for your attention beyond the task(s) at hand: your phone, social media, personal email, coworkers—the list goes on. But cutting through the mental clutter makes for more efficient, stronger work.

1) Set an achievable goal—such as completing a languishing presentation, reorganizing your folders, or putting together a meeting agenda—then focus on it until it's finished.

2) Stash your phone somewhere you can't reach it—or set it on airplane mode.

3) If the office is noisy and you're stuck at your desk, use noise-canceling headphones (see page 65), even if you're not listening to music.

4) Be friendly but firm with chatty colleagues: tell them you can't wait to catch up . . . later.

5) When you start to lose focus, give yourself a timed five-minute break to get up and walk around, then return to what you were working on.

2

EXPRESS
YOURSELF

TAKE EXCELLENT NOTES

Taking notes during meetings is positive for three reasons: it helps you retain what you're hearing, it ensures you'll have a record of the conversation, and it's an easy way to show everyone that you're paying attention.

Here's how to maximize your note-taking skills, whether you use a pen or a keyboard:

1) Start with a clean page. Label it clearly with the date, the participants, and the topic.

2) Create an efficient note-taking format and stick to it for all meetings. Being consistent will make it easier to search and review your notes.

3) Be both concise and thorough. Use lists and abbreviations to help you move quickly without missing anything.

4) Resist the urge to let out your inner Pablo Picasso. Doodling suggests that you aren't very interested in what's being said.

5) Expand your notes postmeeting. Take a few minutes while things are still fresh to expand on points and to identify actionable next steps—just like in college!

6) Make time each week to review your notes. This will help you remember priorities and track progress.

To:
Cc:
Subject:

WRITE AN AMAZING EMAIL:

- Say hello and please.

- Ask to receive urgently needed things "soonest."

- Thank people for their help.*

- Remember that all emails are easily forwarded.

*P.S. Do this even if people may forget to thank you. It doesn't mean they aren't appreciative. (But one-up them and say thanks often.)

WRITE AMAZING EMAILS

Although we send and receive hundreds of emails each week—sometimes every day—thoughtful, impactful correspondence isn't the norm. Instead, names are misspelled, pleasantries are ignored, and punctuation is skipped. But taking extra care with email will strengthen work relationships, both within and beyond your office walls.

To:

Cc:

Subject:

WRITE A TERRIBLE EMAIL:

- Make a demand without an introduction.

- Write "ASAP"—it can read as snappy and stressful.

- Take your coworkers' support for granted and forget to thank them.

- Write anything that you'd never want someone else to see.

AVOID ANGRY EMAILING

Oh, the pissy missive. We're all guilty of penning a few of these, and we've regretted most of them. Angry emails are cathartic, but ideally, they rarely get sent. If an infuriating communication lands in your inbox, go ahead and write a response. But then, instead of pressing send, press save and immediately take a breath. Odds are that in rereading what you wrote, you'll see the need to tone things down.

Keep things cordial, even if it pains you. Email is akin to a permanent marker: once you've sent it, it's very hard to scrub its message clean.

DON'T FORGET THE PHONE

We live in a digital-first culture, and because many of us have never even had a landline, it feels natural to rely almost entirely on text-based communication to connect with people.

But this does a disservice to how personal, efficient, and effective a phone call can be. If you're dealing with a sensitive situation, need an immediate answer, or are building relationships, pick up the phone and call. You'll get the answers you need faster and you'll also establish a real connection with someone. (Bonus: It's harder to say "no" over the phone.)

MAKE A GREAT PRESENTATION

A visual tool like PowerPoint or Keynote lends an air of professionalism to a presentation, so long as you avoid the pitfalls of wacky fonts, tasteless jokes, and distracting animations. (What is it about presentations that makes people go nuts with bad puns?)

1) Limit your presentation to twenty slides or fewer.

2) Select one simple, handsome font.

3) Create an easy-to-follow narrative.

4) Put any key points on-screen as a way to frame your presentation.

5) Don't expect the slides to do all the work. Their job is to punctuate what you're saying.

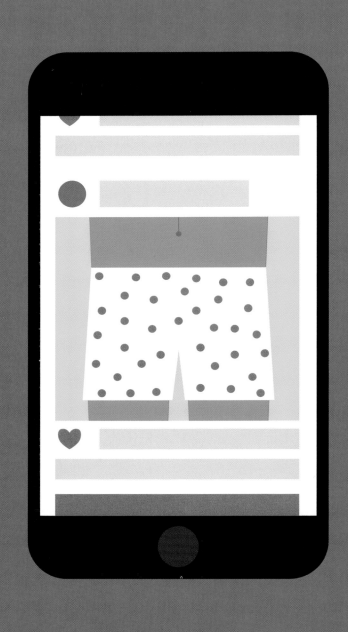

NAVIGATE SOCIAL MEDIA LIKE A BOSS

As some former politicians will tell you, you can destroy your career in 140 characters or fewer. Social media is a powerful tool—and its powers can be used for good or evil.

● The Internet is forever. That means that what you put online is almost impossible to take back. Consider this your guiding star when it comes to your social media content.

● As an employee, you're a representative of your company—in life and online. Know that in the eyes of the public, if you identify your workplace in your profile, you might as well be the company spokesperson.

● Speak positively about your workplace online—or don't talk about it at all. This matters to both your current employer and your future ones.

● For the love of all that's holy: no racy photos. In fact, only post photos that you'd feel okay with your boss—and your future bosses—seeing.

● Social media provides the opportunity to be noticed for all the right reasons. It's a public place for you to be your smartest, wittiest, and savviest self. Crafting an intelligent social media presence will get you noticed and establish you as a thought leader in your field.

3

FOOD, SNACKS, AND THE OFFICE KITCHEN

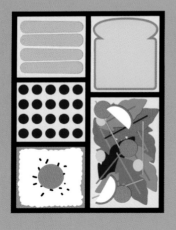

PACK A HEALTHY LUNCH

Take control of your well-being (and budget) by bringing lunch from home—if not every day, then at least a couple of times per week. If you're in need of inspiration, here are some healthy ideas to get you started.

MASON JAR SALADS

These are best assembled with lettuces, assorted vegetables, grains, or pasta. Put the dressing at the bottom of the jar to avoid wilted-salad syndrome.

SANDWICHES

Among the endless options are nut butter and banana on wheat bread, turkey on rye, the no-fail BLT, and a variety of vegetables with mustard and Swiss cheese.

BENTO BOXES

Whether you're packing hummus and vegetables, deconstructed tacos, or a traditional Japanese lunch (rice, fish or meat, and vegetables), a bento box is a visually satisfying and organized way to control portions.

SOUPS

Make a soup on Sunday and you've got lunch until Friday. Pack it in a thermos for easy transport and to prevent spills. (Bonus: Sipping soup leaves one hand free to multitask your way through a working lunch.)

STAY SANE AT THE FREE SNACK BAR

Remember the Freshman 15? Meet its cousin, the Fresh-Job 15. Fight back against free-office-food pounds by choosing snacks in the 100-calorie zone. Here are some ideas that toe the line:

- Infused water, black coffee, and tea (all zero calories and a good place to start)

- A small skim-milk latte

- ½ cup nonfat Greek yogurt

- 25 regular M&M'S or 9 peanut M&M'S

- 1 Reese's Peanut Butter Cup (110 calories and totally worth it)

- 3 small squares of dark chocolate

- 1 small apple or banana with ½ tablespoon peanut butter

- 1 cup berries

- Raw vegetables with 2 tablespoons hummus

- 25 pistachios

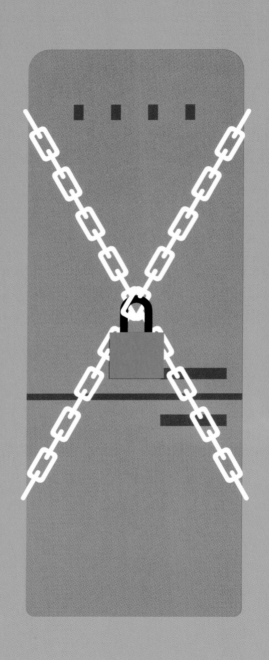

RULES OF THE OFFICE FRIDGE

There's actually only one rule, and it's simple: don't eat anyone else's food. The office fridge can be a hotbed for dramatics, particularly when your lunch goes missing or you unwittingly polish off the birthday girl's last cupcake.

Written directives in the shared fridge can easily veer into the passive aggressive—or straight-up aggressive, e.g. "This yogurt belongs to Dave—not you, so don't eat it." Clearly and simply label your food containers with your name and attach a friendly note to items that need special protection, such as prosecco for a party: "Please don't drink me. I'm needed for an event."

Of course, the white flag in the fridge battle is always the "Please take one!" note. If you've got something to share, say so. Bonus points if it's alcoholic.

WHAT NOT TO
MICROWAVE AT WORK

FISH
That means anything that contains fish or smells like fish.
(Here's looking at you, tuna casserole.)

EGGS
Whoever suggested microwaving an egg in a mug definitely
didn't work in an office.

POPCORN
Burned popcorn, that is. If you're going to make popcorn,
pull the bag from the microwave early or deal with the
consequences. Or, better yet, buy the prepopped stuff.

DRESS UP YOUR DESK LUNCH

If you can't make it to your favorite sit-down restaurant at lunchtime—c'mon, who can?—you can dress up your desk lunch so it looks and feels respectable. Keep a few of these staples within reach for an instant upgrade.

FANCY SALT

MINI PEPPER MILL

HOT SAUCE

GOOD OLIVE OIL

CERAMIC PLATES AND BOWLS

REAL SILVERWARE

COOL GLASSWARE

KEEP IT HEALTHY

A LESSON IN ERGONOMICS

Ergonomics sounds like a college class you might have failed. But it's actually an applied method for arranging things to optimize comfort and reduce stress. You can make your workspace more ergonomic—no special equipment needed—with just a handful of tweaks.

1) First up: no slouching.

2) Keep your arms straight, your wrists relaxed, and desktop items within easy reach.

3) Position your computer screen an arm's length away and at eye level.

4) Stand up, walk around, and change positions at least once every 90 minutes.

DIY STANDING DESK

Scientific studies have linked "sedentary time"—that is, sitting—with obesity, heart disease, and even early death. Jeez. If headlines like "Sitting Is the New Smoking" are enough to make you leap out of your chair and stay there, at least now you know you don't have to buy an expensive standing desk to do it.

● Repurpose your desktop library by placing your laptop on a stack of books.

● A bookshelf can host an elevated workspace.

● Embrace the minimalism of a single-wall shelf—just make sure it's securely mounted.

TEN WAYS TO DE-STRESS AT YOUR DESK

If you find yourself getting worked up—heart racing, feet tapping, temper soaring—take a moment to recenter and diffuse your stress.

1) Grab your headphones and cue up calming music.

2) Put your computer on sleep mode.

3) Swivel away from your desktop and close your eyes.

4) Breathe like you're in yoga class: Extend your breath for a count of four, inhale deeply, and exhale slowly and fully for another four-count. Then repeat.

5) Get up and take a 10-minute walk, preferably outside.

6) Talk to a friend. Briefly touching base with your personal life puts work stress in perspective.

7) Brew yourself a cup of herbal tea.

8) Unclutter your desk (see page 13). Clearing your workspace creates mental space, too.

9) Find someplace discreet (like a stairwell) to do jumping jacks or some other form of quick exercise (see page 59).

10) Make a postwork plan. Whether it's a trip to the gym or a happy-hour cocktail, give yourself something appealing to look forward to.

UNTANGLE YOURSELF FROM OVERCOMMITMENT

Busy is good; overwhelmed is awful. It can contribute to stress and anxiety, as well as a lack of sleep. If you're feeling overcommitted, don't silently tread water while hoping not to be pulled beneath the waves of deadlines.

● Understand team priorities: talk to your supervisor and colleagues about what on your plate is most important.

● Downsize your workload, delegating anything you can to a trusted colleague.

● Negotiate timelines and extend any deadlines that can be shifted.

● Set limits and be honest when you feel you've reached your capacity. This will manage your team's expectations and help preserve your sanity.

WORKING OUT AT WORK

Some lucky people manage to sneak out during lunchtime to hit the gym. If, like us, you have a hard time pulling that off, here's how to sneak in some exercise at the office.

USING THE STAIRS (A)
Banish the elevator and take the stairs.

BOOKS AS WEIGHTS (B)
Improvise a set of five-pound weights with books and use them for bicep curls, front-arm raises, and overhead presses.

PUSH-UPS ON FLOOR OR DESK (C)
No tools required.

SEATED LEG RAISES (D)
Do toning leg raises under your desk.

WALKING AROUND THE OFFICE (E)
Take a lap around the office, whether you're on a call or just need to clear your head.

SQUATS (F)
Ditch your desk chair and do a series of slow squats.

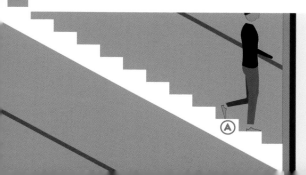

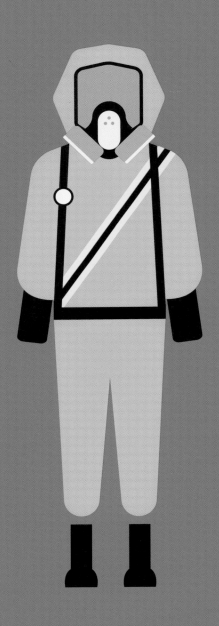

AVOID OFFICE GERMS

The office can be a real petri dish, especially during cold and flu season—or anytime coworkers are under the weather and refuse to call in sick. (They should really stay home.)

1) Get a flu shot. Odds are it's free with your insurance.

2) Wash your hands and buddy up to your hand sanitizer.

3) Try not to touch your eyes, nose, mouth, or anywhere else on your face.

4) Avoid close contact with coworkers.

5) Take extra good care of yourself. Eat well (including vitamin C), sleep well, de-stress, and stay hydrated.

SAVE YOUR EYESIGHT

Computer vision syndrome is a real affliction in which eyestrain is the result of focusing intently on a computer screen for more than two hours at a time. Symptoms include blurred vision, double vision, eye irritation, and headache. Sound familiar?

It's not inevitable! Here are ways to prevent it.

● Use proper screen brightness (not too low, not too high).

● Minimize glare by positioning your screen correctly. If that doesn't work, purchase an antiglare filter.

● Have your computer at the ideal height: when looking straight ahead, your line of sight should align with the top of the monitor.

● Make an effort to blink frequently (this will prevent your eyes from drying out).

● Give your eyes a rest: take a 15-minute break following every two hours of continuous computer use.

INVEST IN THE BEST NOISE-CANCELING HEADPHONES

If you work in a noisy room, noise-canceling headphones are almost a necessity. Consider these factors when looking to drown out the endless saga that is your coworker's dating life.

KNOW THE DIFFERENCE

Noise-canceling headphones use technology to negate the sounds around you, while noise-isolating headphones create a seal around your ears to block sound physically. (The latter are often less expensive—and also less effective and comfortable.)

TEST THE SOUND

Test the headphones by listening to a variety of audio: rock and roll, podcasts, and hip-hop with lots of bass. Listen in silence, then ask people around you to talk and make noise, just like at the office.

CONSIDER COMFORT LEVEL

Noise-canceling headphones can be heavy and clunky, so make sure you try them on before taking the plunge! Leave them on for as long as you can to gauge their comfort level, as you'll likely be reaching for them frequently—and potentially for hours at a time.

PROTECT YOUR INVESTMENT

The good ones are often pricey ($100 plus), but sometimes you can't put a price on productivity. If you do splurge, make sure your headphones have a warranty.

TAKE TIMEOUTS

Taking regular breaks during your workday makes you more effective and focused and keeps you happier. Step away from your desk every 90 minutes to optimize your productivity. (And avoid a vitamin D deficiency by making sure you leave the office for fresh air at least twice daily.)

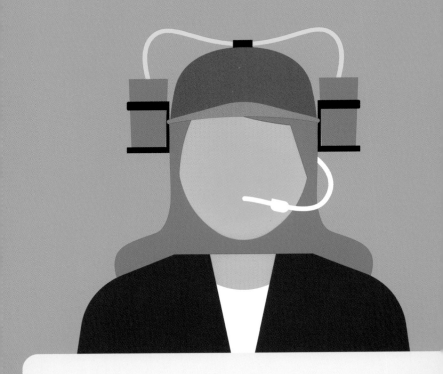

STAY HYDRATED

Drink at least five glasses (about 40 ounces) of water at work per day. Here are as many steps to help you do so:

1) Keep a large water bottle on your desk.

2) Fill it up each morning when you arrive at work.

3) Make things more interesting by adding ice and natural flavor boosters.

4) Fizzy water counts, too.

5) Repeat as needed to get to five glasses per workday. Bonus points if you make it eight.

5

OFFICE CULTURE

DEFINING BUSINESS CASUAL

"Business casual" is an ambiguous dress code that has traditionally included khakis, collared shirts, sport coats, blouses, and dresses. But that harks back to a time when denim was still a dirty word at the office. These days, the meaning of business casual varies wildly from one office to the next, and your workplace's particular interpretation will become clear after a week or two of being there. Until then, you usually can't go wrong with a clean, crisp shirt, black or dark jeans, and smart-looking shoes.

If you're not sure about an outfit's workplace acceptability, ask yourself this: Can you attend an off-site meeting in these clothes and still feel like a positive representative of your company? When in doubt, err on the side of formal. No one has ever lost an opportunity because they were overdressed.

HOW TO BEHAVE
AT OFFICE PARTIES

The office party presents a minefield of opportunities, both good and bad. Although your office mates are likely to be dressed in party clothes and enjoying free booze—and, hopefully—mini sliders, it's important to remember that a work party is still work.

Here's some advice that will prevent you from waking up and wondering if you should quit on the spot.

GO
Skipping the office party can send the wrong message. Give your coworkers a chance to know you, whether you're meeting for the first time or just talking about something other than, say, spreadsheets.

NETWORK
Use the event as a chance to meet colleagues you otherwise don't interact with every day, including management and executive staff.

DRINK WITHIN YOUR LIMITS
Boring? No such thing when the alternative is company-wide embarrassment. Loosen up a bit, but keep your wits about you, your words in check—and your pants on.

AVOID SNARK—AND FIGHTS
Keep your conversations light and interesting. Avoid the awkwardness of bickering with someone you may not speak to again until the next work event (for example, don't try to feed the hardcore vegan a mini slider).

FITTING INTO THE COMPANY CULTURE

Whether it's fair or not, "culture fit"—how well your values, interests, and style align with your colleagues'—plays a big part in getting ahead at work, sometimes even over other marks of success. So what do you do if the office vibe feels foreign to you? Before you read what follows, ask yourself if culture fit is something you want to work on. If not, start looking for new opportunities elsewhere.

IDENTIFY YOUR DEAL BREAKERS
Maybe replying to after-dark emails isn't a big thing to you, but going out with coworkers several nights a week is. Decide what you absolutely can't deal with and set boundaries, then identify the areas you can work on.

MAKE AN EFFORT
Just because you're a dog person in an office full of cat people, you can still be on good terms with them. Engage with coworkers, be friendly, and join them for social outings often enough so as not to seem standoffish.

BE YOURSELF
At the end of the day, the only thing you can be is yourself. Taking a conscious approach to culture fit can be productive, but only so long as you stay true to who you are.

GIVING GIFTS AT WORK

It's fair to say that gifts at work are never mandatory, though a written card to mark an occasion—a birthday, a holiday, a wedding—is thoughtful and appreciated. If you do choose to purchase gifts for coworkers, consider buying only for your boss. (Beyond that, either include everyone on your team or be covert about it to ensure no one feels left out.) Here are a few thoughts on selecting gifts with a supervisor in mind:

• Keep it neutral. Don't gift anything too personal, like a scarf you've knitted. Instead, select something that registers as a thoughtful gesture, such as a favorite book or bottle of wine, fancy hand soaps, or a gift card for a local coffee shop.

• Don't overspend. A high-ticket item is likely to make your boss uncomfortable.

• Whenever possible, include a gift receipt—a classy move that allows for discreet returns and exchanges.

• Don't expect a gift in return. If the exchange isn't mutual, it may mean your boss isn't into the ritual and that a card is a better choice next time.

BE THE BEST OFFICE DJ

If you have access to the office playlist, first appreciate the power that you hold and then pick music that neither bums out your colleagues nor makes them go silently insane.

THE SAFE ZONE:
Nineties R&B
Motown
(Upbeat) indie
Top 40
Reggae
Classic rock

POLARIZING—PROCEED WITH CAUTION:
Very sad emo
Reclusive one-hit wonders
Heavy metal
Expletive-laden rap
EDM
Contemporary country

HANDLE FREE BOOZE
(RESPONSIBLY)

Whether it comes in the form of a tucked-away bottle of bourbon, a fridge stocked with beer, or an on-site Jägermeister Shotmeister, free alcohol can be an office perk. If it's after-hours and offered, by all means imbibe. But here's the tricky part: don't get drunk. Tipsy? Eh. But drunk? Never.

This can be complicated, depending on your office culture and the availability of food. Your workplace is never really going to be a bar, even when the sun goes down.

RUN THE OFFICE
BETTING POOL

Despite their popularity, the legality of Super Bowl, Oscars, and March Madness office pools can be murky—that is, assuming you're playing for money and not for free meals or company swag. (We feel compelled to say that playing for swag is a solid option.)

Here's how to run an office pool—and stay out of hot water:

1) Check with HR to make sure there is no company-wide ban on gambling of any kind.

2) Keep the pool small and the buy-in low ($5 to $10 is a good amount).

3) Set up simple rules, like a fillable bracket or box pool.

4) Track everyone's picks neatly—and confidentially—on a spreadsheet.

5) Don't pay yourself for managing the pool. Profiting from a betting pool is both illegal and will make you look cheap.

TALKING POLITICS (OR NOT!) AT WORK

Given what's going on in the world these days, political discussions are often unavoidable—and can be heated. And because we spend so much time with our coworkers, those potentially spirited conversations will inevitably come up at work. In the company of friends, it's easy to get into a shouting match over political views (and sometimes it's a fight worth having).

But navigating opposing views at work requires treading lightly. If you find yourself at odds with a coworker, use your disagreement as an opportunity to learn about his or her stance. It's unlikely you're going to change your coworker's mind, and the office—or the after-work bar—isn't the right place to try. The phrase "we'll have to agree to disagree" was made for these moments: respectfully hear him or her out and then let it go.

SHARING A BATHROOM
(OR HOW TO POOP AT WORK)

Let's address that thing that everyone wants to know but nobody wants to talk about. That thing is pooping at work and hiding the smell, which can be especially horrifying (for everyone involved) with a shared bathroom. Keep things copacetic by following a few simple rules.

THE COURTESY FLUSH
A well-timed flush (that is, immediately after you're finished) helps minimize odor because it doesn't give it a chance to dissipate. Up your game by flushing as you go (a move we like to call Courtesy Flush 2.0).

THE SINK FULL OF BUBBLES
If you're in a single-stall bathroom, squirt some soap into the sink and run the water before you get started. This will fill the room with a soapy smell that'll combat any unwanted odors.

THE SCENT BARRIER IN THE BOWL
Essential oils or a specially formulated spray like Poo-Pourri creates a scent barrier that lives on the top of the toilet bowl water. Add some drops or a spritz to the bowl before you go.

LEAVE THE MATCHES AT HOME
Setting off the fire alarm isn't worth it, we promise.

WORK RELATIONSHIPS

MAKING WORK FRIENDS

Making friends at the office can turn a good job into a great gig. But building these relationships can take a little time, and some strategizing.

1) Make the first move. Cut to the chase and be the first to introduce yourself.

2) Be positive, and helpful. Establish yourself as a trust-worthy coworker (see page 97).

3) Find common ground. Pay attention to what your future friend likes (or hates). Point out any similarities you share.

4) Take your time. Friendships often unfold slowly, so don't overwhelm your new pal with too much attention.

5) Get together outside the office. Grab a coffee, lunch, or a drink and talk about your lives away from work and about how you can help each other on the job.

WORKING WITH YOUR "REAL" FRIENDS

Since many job opportunities are often circulated through employees' personal connections, good friends can easily end up working in the same office. Fun! And frequently complicated!

1) When referring friends for jobs at your company, do so based on their potential to be a professional asset. That means, only recommend friends who you've seen do great work. The same things that make someone an awesome friend, like being spontaneous and slapstick funny, don't always translate into being an awesome employee.

2) Set some boundaries in advance. Before you start working together, make a plan to maintain distance between your personal and professional relationships. A petty disagreement outside of work should never find its way into the office.

3) Foster your separate professional identities. Avoid falling into the "work bestie" zone with your real-life pal. It can be detrimental for your coworkers to view you two as one and the same. You'll likely have different lives at work, and that's okay. It's more of an indication of professional growth than trouble on the friendship front.

BE A TRUSTED COWORKER

Gaining your colleagues' trust is a long game, and it's one worth winning. Prove that you're a trustworthy confidant by being a thoughtful, active listener as well as a steel trap: don't share what you're told with anyone else at the office, unless the information is potentially damaging to your colleague, the company, or other coworkers. In short, keep secrets—and don't talk shit.

HOW TO FIND A MENTOR

A great professional mentor can impart valuable wisdom and experience—and provide access to new opportunities that help advance your career. But how do you find one and how do you convince your choice to take you under his or her wing?

1) Check out your options. Who in your office do you really admire? An ideal mentor is someone with a work ethic and position to which you aspire.

2) Look beyond your department. Your mentor doesn't have to work in the same realm to be inspiring. Admired experts outside of your specialty can offer fresh perspective.

3) Reach out and say hi. Flattery works, we promise. Write an email saying you admire his or her work ethic and career and would love to get together to learn from him or her. Maximize the opportunity. When you meet, ask specific questions that draw on the person's experience. This is an effective way to get direct, useful information, and he or she will be flattered you did your research.

4) Make your prospective mentor's job easy. Be thoughtful, grateful, and punctual when you see each other.

FALLING IN LOVE AT WORK

Welcome to this hornet's nest! Casually sleeping with your coworker(s) is a nightmarishly bad idea. It has the potential to make your workplace chaotic and puts both your professional reputation and your job at risk.

But falling in love with a coworker? Well, there may be something to it. You've got similar jobs, stuff in common, and lots to talk about . . . at least in regard to work. Our best advice is this: Take. It. Slowly. Now repeat that. Spend platonic time together outside of work, introduce him or her around to your friends, and, most important, think on this a lot. The harmony of your workplace, where you spend the majority of your time, is on the line.

If you dive into a relationship with a colleague, make sure you can envision yourself investing in it—and potentially leaving your position, if needed. Depending on the circumstances (for example, if your partner is your boss), getting serious may mean leaving the company.

AVOIDING UNWANTED ROMANTIC ATTENTION

Receiving unwanted romantic attention from a colleague is a whole different kind of problem, and is one to be taken seriously. The first three steps that follow apply to being casually approached by an interested party. If it's anything more serious, skip immediately to Step 4.

1) Avoid the potential for mixed signals by coolly deflecting all compliments and advances.

2) Discuss only work-centric topics. Decline all invitations to socialize outside of work.

3) If the above steps don't work, tackle the situation head-on: say you value your working relationship but have no interest in anything beyond that.

4) If you feel like you're being harassed, report it to your supervisor and/or human resources. They can file a claim and move through established processes to ensure the behavior stops quickly.

STAYING COOL
AND SAVING FACE

SETTING BOUNDARIES

Your workload is like a goldfish: it'll grow to fill the space it's given. It may be that the office culture you're walking into has expectations that are nonnegotiable, like working the occasional evening and weekend and keeping your phone within reach. You have a small window at the start of each new job to set boundaries—and it's worth doing.

● Stay late when absolutely necessary, but otherwise leave at a normal hour. Be a high achiever during set business hours, then go home and decompress.

● Always answer important emails on receipt, but don't answer nonurgent ones at all hours. Save those for the normal workday. Your coworkers should get the hint that you're not on call 24/7.

● Protect your weekends (and your colleagues' too). Don't use Saturday mornings to catch up on emails, which can be stressful to your coworkers and signals that you're always plugged in.

HOW TO ARGUE AT WORK

You know what isn't a good look? Getting into a screaming match in the office. Here's how to win disagreements without raising your voice.

1) Understand the other perspective.

2) Don't shout, use profanity, or call anyone names.

3) Attack the idea, not the person.

4) Use lots of solid evidence.

5) Explain how you feel.

6) Know when to stand down.

HANDLE THE CONDESCENDING COWORKER

Dealing with a patronizing colleague can be infuriating. Because condescension plus retaliation is a perfect recipe for an office blowup, here are some thoughts on declawing the interaction.

First, determine if your colleague is actually talking down to you. It may be that he or she is just generally stressed and lashing out. If you're not sure, check for the following signs: shouting, personal insults, and excessive snark.

From there, you have a few choices:

- Ignore it. Take a deep breath and shrug it off.

- Redirect the bad energy by saying something like, "I'd be happy to do that for you. Can you just share a little more information to help me understand?"

- Confront it directly. Tell your colleague that you feel as though you are being spoken to in a condescending way and that you'd like to get to the bottom of the problem.

- Speak to your supervisor. If you've tried the above to no avail, ask your boss to mediate in a conversation between you and the coworker.

PREVENT LAZY PEOPLE
FROM PASSING THEIR WORK ON TO YOU

Let's talk about one of the trickiest coworkers around: the kind who secretly tries to make you do his or her work. This situation sucks! But first, here's a checklist:

1) Is the work you're being asked to do actually your job?

2) Is the offending colleague noticeably overwhelmed?

3) Do you have a lot of spare time at work?

Answered "no" to all three? Okay, let's strategize.

1) Address the action face-to-face: ask your coworker what's up. If he or she is really in a jam, help come up with a way to redistribute the work so it gets done.

2) If the ask is inappropriate, it's perfectly okay to politely say no. Explain that you already have a full plate of priorities.

3) If that doesn't work, check with your supervisor. Being transparent with your boss isn't the same as ratting out your colleague. Explain the situation and ask if it's okay to shift your energies toward this new workload. (The likely response? No.)

YOU MADE A HUGE MISTAKE. NOW WHAT?

If you've fucked up royally and are unable to remedy the situation, stay calm, quickly seek out your boss, and—once she or he is sitting down—be completely honest and transparent about what went down.

1) Explain it—how the mistake happened and how you've strategized to fix it—and then ask for assistance in making the next move.

2) Own it: apologize, accept all responsibility, and don't be defensive or try to cast the blame on others.

3) Get over it: assure your colleagues that you've learned from this and that it'll never happen again.

By embracing the mistake, you'll help ensure that you and your team can leave this issue behind.

UNDERSTANDING ELECTRONIC PRIVACY

Your work computer isn't your personal property, which means nothing you do on that thing can be considered private. NOTHING! Your company, and your boss, has the right to access your browser history, your work emails, and, in the case of your company-issued cell phone, your call log and your text messages. Even office tools like Slack don't provide a safe haven for speaking frankly at work.

But don't panic just yet. The rigors of electronic surveillance vary by industry and company, and it's unlikely that your boss is reading all of your emails. That said, you should still behave as if it's happening. Have private, sensitive—or scandalous—conversations in person or on the phone. If you can afford it, buy your own cell phone rather than use a company-owned one. And while you can dance like no one is watching, be sure to behave on the office Internet like everyone is.

THE BOSS

TRUTHS ABOUT YOUR BOSS

We don't know your boss, but we have some educated guesses as to what she or he is up against. We hope that you work for someone who is patient and thoughtful, who describes tasks in full detail, and who always prioritizes your need to be intellectually stimulated. But here's the universal truth: work is crazy, deadlines are crazy, and managing a team can also be—you guessed it—pretty crazy. So if your boss isn't always a beacon of professionalism and life goals, consider the following:

● Your boss is under pressure, whether from internal or from outside forces, like her or his own boss.

● Your boss can't do it all alone. And that is intimidating.

● Your boss wants to trust you. (Even if the opposite feels true, and you feel micromanaged.)

● Your boss has likely done your job before—or something close to it. She or he came up through the ranks, too, and understands how you feel.

● Your boss is grateful for you, even if that gratitude is not always properly expressed.

● Your boss may never tell you any of this. That doesn't mean she or he doesn't want to.

BE INDISPENSABLE

This is sound advice not only in regard to your boss but to your whole team.

● Drink the Kool-Aid. Believe in your workplace; be a champion of the cause.

● Be a team player. Know that you're all in it together, and work to get shared goals accomplished.

● Actively make your boss's job easier. Show your supervisor that you understand him or her.

● Offer extra help when it's needed—even if it's inconvenient.

● Be a problem solver. Strive to offer a solution whenever issues arise.

● Learn new skills and share them. Expanding your expertise—and sharing your knowledge with others—makes you more valuable as an employee.

● Be honest. Always. Your coworkers will seek you out for your opinion.

● Maintain a good sense of humor, even (especially!) when things get tricky.

● Be someone people can count on, whether it's for a walk to get coffee or a serious chat.

DISAGREE WITH YOUR BOSS

Good supervisors value the opinions of the people they work with—as long as they're well researched and presented in the right way. Disagreeing with your boss can be productive for you both, but keep in mind a few things.

1) First, build trust. Take time in your working relationship to establish a strong rapport with your boss. Your opinions are more likely to be taken seriously if your relationship is one of mutual respect.

2) Never disagree with your boss in front of other people, whether clients or coworkers. Doing so can (correctly) be interpreted as a sign of disrespect.

3) Be tactful. Make it clear that you respect your boss's position, but that you want to raise a point he or she may not have yet considered.

4) Know when to stand down. Voicing your opinion doesn't mean you're going to change your boss's mind.

5) Respect and support the final decision, regardless of whose idea it was.

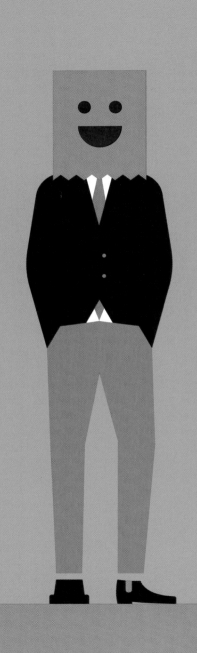

WORKING WITH
A BOSS YOU HATE

Luckily, there's a difference between liking someone and respecting someone. Can't stand the person in charge? You can still respect your boss for his or her expertise. Don't let one individual ruin a great gig.

● Keep your nose to the grindstone. Be excellent at what you do. It can help catch the attention of other senior-level people at the company.

● Kill your boss with kindness, even if you have to go into robot mode to do it.

● Be honest with yourself. Are you doing anything to provoke your boss's behavior? (If so, fix it.)

● Keep a record. If your boss is totally unreasonable, keep his or her emails and a log of offenses. If things come to a head, you'll have evidence that you've been mistreated.

● Celebrate your wins! Don't let your crappy boss get in the way of you feeling great about what you've accomplished.

A LESSON FROM TEFLON

Teflon is a nonstick coating that keeps pans from wearing the scars of cooking adventures gone wrong. When it comes to "Shit Your Boss Says," try to take on your own fluorocarbon veneer. A boss's frustration can manifest itself into barbed, semi-insulting exchanges, and supervisors have a special way of forgetting their outbursts—likely because they're embarrassing. Let heat-of-the-moment snappiness roll off your back. Carrying those moments around creates emotional residue that you don't need. (They're no more important than yesterday morning's burned pancakes.)

MEETINGS

GET OUT OF
UNNECESSARY MEETINGS

At any given time, millions of people in offices all around the world are having pointless meetings—work that could have been accomplished in an email. It's time to push back.

• If you don't know what a pending meeting is for, don't automatically accept the calendar invite. Ask what your role will be in the meeting before you say yes.

• Request an agenda. A thoughtful agenda, circulated in advance, will illustrate how much needs to be discussed—and if the meeting is warranted.

• Offer an alternative use of your time. If you doubt that you're needed in the meeting, offer another way for you to spend your time that could be more productive. Example: "I'm aiming to get this report done by the end of the day. I could use this hour to work on that, unless you think it's best for me to attend the meeting."

HOW TO CONDUCT YOURSELF IN VIDEO CONFERENCES

Approach a video conference the same way you would a regular meeting: rested, well prepared, and ready to talk. Before the conference begins, familiarize yourself with the technology. Check that the camera works and is angled to face you. Test the microphone to make sure you're seated close enough to be heard. Is the lighting bright enough? Is there an empty lunch container or other trash "in the shot" that might be distracting? Once you've established the connection, speak clearly and naturally and engage with other participants by practicing active listening (nodding, smiling) and by looking directly into the camera.

STAY FOCUSED AND ENGAGED IN LONG MEETINGS

We've all been there: digging our fingernails into our palms to avoid falling asleep in what seems like a never-ending meeting. Long meetings are rarely more productive than short ones, but they're inevitable. Keep it together by arriving well rested, caffeinated, and having eaten something. Both actively taking notes (see page 25) and participating in the conversation will help keep you engaged in the meeting. If you find your attention lagging, excuse yourself from the room and get your blood pumping with a short, brisk walk. (Ducking out briefly is infinitely less embarrassing than passing out on the conference table.)

OWN THE
CONFERENCE ROOM

BE A LEADER
Come prepared, and help guide the conversation so it remains efficient and worthwhile.

HAVE AN AGENDA
A list of specific points that you want to cover will help move the conversation forward.

BE AT EASE
You're in the company of colleagues with shared goals, so there's no reason to be nervous.

KEEP IT BRIEF
Don't talk for the sake of talking. Stay on task and help others to do the same.

FOLLOW UP
Even if you didn't take in-depth notes, send around main takeaways from the meeting to everyone who attended.

10

OUT OF THE OFFICE:
VACATIONS AND SICK DAYS

PUTTING IN THE REQUEST

The best strategy for requesting time off is to do it both confidently and as early as possible. As soon as your vacation plans begin to take shape, email your supervisor with the dates you want to be away. It can be helpful to include a plan that details how your duties will be covered while you're gone, and to highlight when you'll get necessary work done in advance. Once your time off has been approved, send your boss a calendar invite that includes the dates, to ensure your well-deserved vacation stays on his or her radar.

JACKPOT

BAR

BAR

WRITING THE "OUT OF OFFICE" MESSAGE

Some people view the Out of Office (OOO) message as an opportunity to gleefully detail their distance from work: "I am on a tropical beach, probably drinking a Corona, and NOT CHECKING EMAIL!" Yes, that will get your point across, but since you don't know who'll be receiving that message while you're gone, it's best to stick politely to the basics: you're away from your desk and aren't regularly checking messages; the date you'll be back; and who to contact in your absence. Make a plan with a colleague before you leave and include her or his contact info in your OOO. (And don't forget to turn off the OOO when you return.)

HOW TO WORK
(OR NOT) FROM AFAR

We're big advocates of unplugging as much as possible while on vacation. If you have a trusted colleague covering your desk during your absence—and it's a quiet week—tune out and never look back.

If things are a bit less settled at the office, it can be anxiety inducing to go a week without knowing what's going on. A good method of balancing work and play while on vacation is to check email at set times twice per day, once in the morning and once at night, Wi-Fi permitting. This way you'll have a sense of how things are going without getting dragged away from the fun.

WORKING REMOTELY (AND EFFICIENTLY)

When working remotely—whether from an airplane, a foreign country, or your couch—the best way to maximize productivity is to create a designated work zone. Set a hard start time to your day, whether you're decamping to your kitchen table or a coffee shop; wear "real" clothes (that is, no pajamas); and make sure you have access to Wi-Fi and power outlets. If you're working in a different time zone from your office, consider altering your working hours to line up with your coworkers' as best you can. (Of course, this can be a bit crazy if you're on the other side of the world.)

PLAYING CATCH-UP AFTER VACATION

The night before returning to work after a vacation can feel like the Sunday-Night Blues on steroids. Avoid the anxiety with a return strategy. (Keep in mind that arriving with snacks or souvenirs from your travels is always considered a baller move by grateful colleagues.)

1) Start the day with an energizing breakfast (or at least a large coffee).

2) Arrive early to the office. Having the place to yourself will allow you to tackle your inbox quickly.

3) Catch up with coworkers first thing. Find out what needs your immediate attention.

4) Make a to-do list. Highlight the priorities, then tackle them thoughtfully and thoroughly.

5) Leave the office on time. Pace yourself: you're not going to make up a week's worth of work in a single day.

HOW TO CALL IN SICK
(WHEN YOU'RE ACTUALLY SICK)

If you're feeling under the weather to the point that it'll interrupt your work or put your colleagues at risk, by all means, stay home. When calling in sick, send your team an early-morning email saying you're sick and suggesting a plan to meet any urgent deadlines, either from home or with the assistance of a coworker. Writing early allows everyone time to strategize how to work around your absence.

Beyond that, drink plenty of fluids, get lots of rest, and keep your strength up.

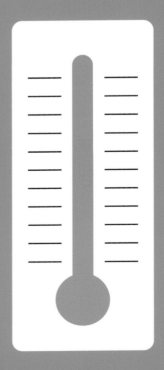

HOW TO CALL IN SICK
(WHEN YOU AREN'T EVEN A LITTLE BIT SICK)

If you're perfectly healthy but need to take a day off, it's best to take a personal day. But sometimes you need to dodge work and stay completely under the radar, particularly when interviewing for another job. And particularly when the timing is inconvenient.

We've worked in environments where supervisors assume "having the flu" means "printing my résumé." Since that isn't fair to the Actually Infirmed, do your part to prove them wrong (and make Ferris Bueller proud).

1) Set the stage. Excuse yourself early the day prior, and make sure people see you do it.

2) Reference your early exit when you write your team the next morning by saying, "I'm sorry, but I still haven't kicked this cold and need to stay home today."

3) Stick to your story. Don't race up the stairs on your return to the office. Instead, say you're still feeling a bit under the weather but are much better.

4) Do not reveal your sneaky self to anyone at work.

5) Don't do this all the time. The fake-out move works best once every few months. If you have multiple interviews, you're going to have to broaden your excuses. (Next time, blame it on the cable guy and come in late.)

11

THE TOUGH STUFF

CRYING AT WORK

Crying at work is awkward, jarring, potentially damaging to your professional reputation—and bound to happen at some point. If it can be helped, discreet crying is always the way to go. (Openly sobbing—especially with frequency—makes your colleagues uncomfortable and can be viewed as unprofessional.)

● Divert your thoughts to stave off crying until you are in a private place.

● Grab your phone or—even better—your laptop.

● Find a spot with a door that closes and locks. A bathroom stall is a tried-and-true hideout.

● Once you have found privacy, give yourself time to recover. Stay busy by answering emails remotely while you collect yourself.

● Excuse yourself for the day if necessary. Personal days exist for a reason, so if you can't regain your composure, go home. (And come back strong the next day.)

GRIEVING AT WORK
(WHEN YOU'VE LOST SOMEONE)

Losing someone you love makes your whole world stop—and then it shifts its axis. Going back to work while grieving lies somewhere on a hard spectrum between Extremely Challenging and Absolutely Impossible. Here are some thoughts on grief at work.

TAKE THE TIME YOU NEED

Go on bereavement leave, then check in with yourself. Is getting dressed and going to work an overwhelming thought? If so, speak honestly with your boss. It's likely that he or she will be happy to allow you some extra days to work from home and ease back into your job.

LET SOME PEOPLE IN

When you go back to work, no one will be expecting you to be "over" what happened to you. Be kind and forgiving with yourself, honest with your boss, and open with trusted coworkers. They all want to be there for you, and help you, even if they don't know exactly how to do it. You can show them the way.

BREAK LARGE TASKS INTO SMALL BITES

If an approaching deadline is overwhelming, divide up the work into manageable pieces. Checking them off your to-do list will keep you on track and moving forward. If you need help from a teammate to get the job done, just ask.

GRIEVING AT WORK
(WITH SOMEONE WHO IS GRIEVING)

ACKNOWLEDGE THE LOSS

It can be hard to know where to begin when someone you work with is hurting. Avoiding the topic can make the person feel more isolated than he or she already does, so start small. Saying "I'm so sorry for your loss, and I want to be helpful to you" is a great place to begin.

BE AN ACTIVE LISTENER

Being available to talk is a compassionate offering for someone who is grieving. Even if you don't know what to say or can't relate to what your coworker is experiencing, lend an ear, and your lunch break.

OFFER YOUR ADVICE, BUT ONLY IF ASKED

Avoid offering unsolicited advice, as it can be perceived in ways you don't intend. If your colleague asks for your opinion, share it, but do so through a lens of compassion. (Now is not the time for tough love.)

BREAKING UP
WITH A COWORKER

Breaking up is famously hard to do. Breaking up with a coworker is a hundred times harder.

- Focus on your work. Think about the job at hand, and your future—as it pertains to your professional goals.

- Don't gossip. Avoid making your colleagues uncomfortable by leaving them in the dark, where they belong.

- Be scarce, and be professional. Scale back on your interactions with your office ex as much as you can while still doing your job. Work to view him or her strictly as a colleague, rather than as someone who has hurt you.

- Fight with your ex on your own time. If you need to share your thoughts in person, do so far away from the office.

- Stay the course. Think long and hard before rekindling the relationship. An on-again, off-again union is poison for the workplace.

DEALING WITH
THE "BAD APPLE"

The saying "one bad apple can ruin the whole bunch" is actually true. One toxic coworker—who trashes other colleagues, complains constantly, and doesn't hesitate to throw you under the bus—can have a similar effect on the workplace. In our experience, the Bad Apple is (often) eventually fired, but you have to live with this disruptive individual in the meantime. (Unfortunately, sometimes the Bad Apple doesn't go anywhere. Sorry.)

● Minimize your contact. Being scarce but pleasant is a good strategy for avoiding negative run-ins.

● Don't waste time discussing the Bad Apple with others. Focus instead on expanding your relationships with the colleagues you like.

● Talk to the troublemaker directly. Calmly confront the situation head-on by explaining that you value the working relationship you share and want to improve it.

● Avoid email. This is a good tactic for dealing with anyone you don't fully trust. Keep interactions face-to-face—that way, the Bad Apple won't have anything concrete to use against you. (However, keep any damning emails he or she sends your way in case you need backup.)

12

MOVING ON UP

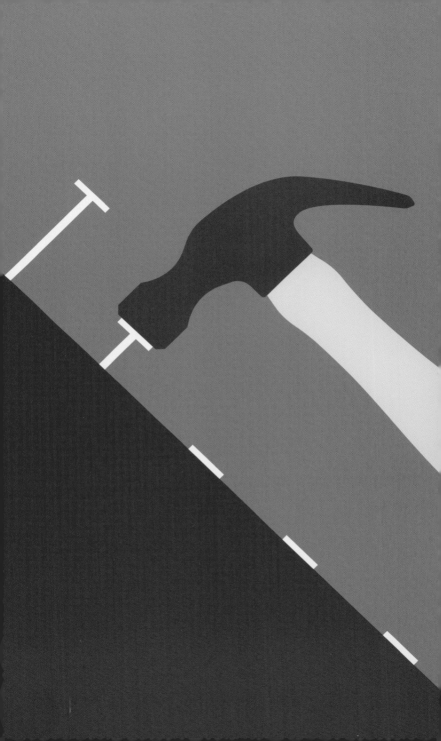

NAIL A PERFORMANCE REVIEW

Regular feedback at work can be hard to come by, which is why your annual performance review is an opportunity to showcase—and reaffirm—how valuable you are.

1) A few months before meeting with your boss, conduct an honest review of yourself, looking at all the ways you've helped advance company goals. If there are weak spots, address them at this time.

2) Prior to your review, create a detailed, organized list of your achievements. Bring two copies to the meeting, one for you and one for your boss.

3) Be receptive to feedback, good and bad.

4) Speak directly and honestly about what goals you want to accomplish in the coming year and what support you need to achieve them.

5) Thank your boss for taking the time to meet with you. Constructive criticism is a catalyst for growth—even if it makes you feel like squirming.

WHEN AND HOW
TO ASK FOR A RAISE

You work hard, you've gamely taken on new challenges, and you've expanded your role in the past year. It sounds like it's time to revisit your compensation (aka you deserve a fat raise). Initiating this conversation is important—and so is how you go about it.

NAIL THE TIMING
Start this conversation at the beginning of the new year, when budgets are malleable, or the anniversary of your start date. Do some reconnaissance with trusted coworkers to gauge what's ideal.

REACH OUT
Send your boss a thoughtful note asking to schedule some time to chat. Example: "Hi: I would like to sit down with you to talk about my progress this year. I am happy to make myself available any time that works for you."

COME PREPARED
Be ready to talk about your accomplishments confidently. Highlight your wins—major projects completed, successful initiatives you've started—and how they've benefited the company. Weave in positive feedback from other people.

DON'T BE VAGUE
Make sure you actually request the raise. Example: "I've given it my all this year and feel that my accomplishments reflect that. In light of this, I'd like to revisit my compensation."

HAVE A CONTINGENCY PLAN
If your boss says that the raise isn't possible, find out when you can expect to revisit the conversation, then hold your boss to it. If salary isn't on the table at all, ask to renegotiate other benefits, like tuition reimbursement—a great opportunity to learn new skills—or more paid time off.

THE INTERNAL TRANSFER:
CHANGING JOBS WITHIN YOUR COMPANY

It's up to you to cultivate your own opportunities, and orchestrating a move within your company can be one example of that. If a great gig opens up at work, go for it. Most organizations are happy to promote from within. But the lateral move requires strategizing.

1) Have you had your current role for at least one year? Some companies won't let you move around if you've been there for less than that.

2) Be transparent with your supervisor. A boss who's interested in your career will be supportive of your interest in the new role, and appreciative of your honesty.

3) Prepare for the interview just as you would if it was a new company. In-house candidates often underprepare, wrongly assuming the role is theirs to lose. (Overprepare and wow your boss instead.)

4) If you get the role, help your team with the transition, even if it means doubling up on duties for a few days.

FREELANCING
WHILE EMPLOYED

Freelancing on top of your regular job lets you build your skill set, portfolio, contacts, bank account, and personal brand. It's also a serious exercise in time management.

The key to freelancing successfully is setting realistic deadlines and carving out the necessary time to meet them, without falling behind in your first priority, your day job.

One early-morning hour before work and one evening hour before bed equal 10 hours during the workweek set aside for freelance projects. If you can spare another five hours during the weekend, you've set aside 15 hours each week to devote to extra projects.

13

THE EXIT

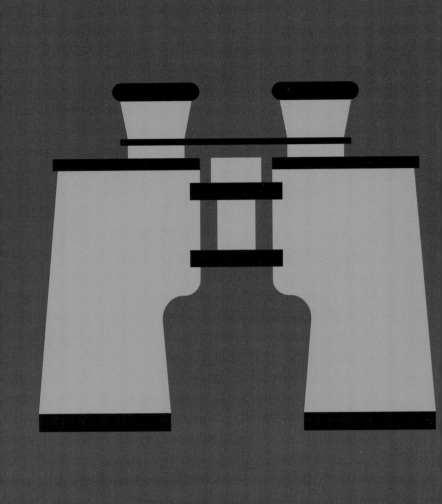

FIND A NEW JOB
(WHILE STILL AT YOUR CURRENT ONE)

The best time to explore new job opportunities is while you're employed, when you're part of an active network. But your search should be discreet. (Bosses don't like the idea of their employees looking to leave, so it's best to keep them entirely in the dark.)

● Update your LinkedIn profile so it's current and inviting to prospective employers.

● Search job sites outside of business hours and never on your work computer. (Consider bringing in your personal laptop and using it on your lunch break if you need to search midday.)

● Tell only your close friends and family about the search. Keep the news off of social media and away from coworkers.

● Reach out only to contacts you trust, and ask them to keep things confidential.

● Schedule interviews early in the morning or late in the afternoon to avoid detection (see page 153).

● No matter what, speak only positively about your current job. Example: "It's been a wonderful learning experience, but I am looking forward to a new challenge."

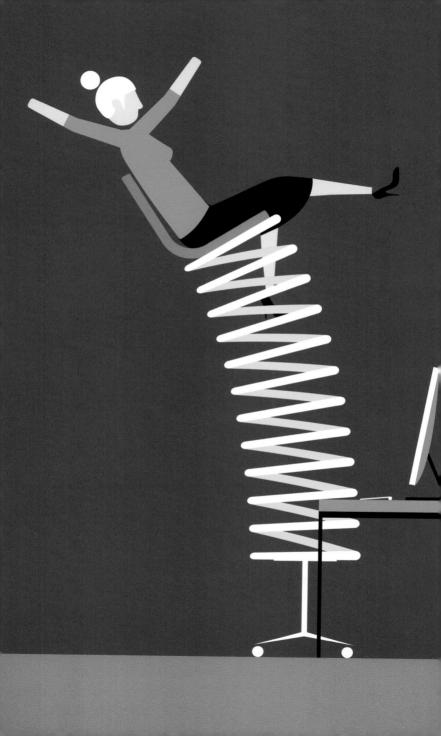

RESIGN (OR GET FIRED) GRACEFULLY

Leaving a job provides an opportunity to make a final, lasting impression at work. Doing it well says a lot about who you are as a professional.

WHEN QUITTING

Once you've received a written offer for a desired new position—or have firmly made up your mind to leave—schedule time with your boss to speak in person. Calmly explain why you're leaving, highlight all you've learned in your role, and offer an exit plan. Two weeks' notice is standard; offering more is appreciated. Also, unless you've been seriously wronged at work, remain positive in your HR exit interview. It's likely that your boss will read a transcript of it, and diplomacy will allow you to use your supervisor as a reference in the future.

WHEN BEING FIRED

Regardless of how it feels to be axed, avoid lashing out at your boss, verbally or—obviously—physically. (This is definitely not the time to serve your boss a cake with the words "I Quit" written in icing.) Instead, approach the conversation as a learning experience: listen, make polite counterpoints as needed, and seek to understand what comes next. Ask about severance, the plan for your last day, and how to communicate the news to your colleagues. If HR isn't present during this conversation, schedule time to talk to your representative immediately. He or she can help walk you through the process.

WRITE AN EXIT MEMO

Exit memos are often required—and always appreciated —when leaving a company. An exit memo is a thorough guide, penned by you, to doing your job. It'll become a bible for your replacement—and a saving grace for whoever fills your role.

Writing one can feel overwhelming, so tackle it in pieces:

1) How you view the job, and how it fits in your company.

2) Where to find all the necessary documents.

3) Contact information for all the critical people.

4) A checklist of tasks to follow each day.

5) Anything else that was a key to your success at that desk.

Save your memo on a shared drive, and print out a clearly labeled hard copy for easy access.

WHAT TO DO
ON YOUR LAST DAY

Your last day on the job gives your colleagues one final impression of you—and it's often the one that sticks. So be gracious, and grateful, and leave all the healthy work relationships intact.

On your last day, wake up, put on something great, and head to the office.

1) Arrive on time and finish any remaining work.

2) Organize your contacts and send them a note about your departure. Example: "Dear All: Today is my last day at Office X, and it's been such a pleasure working with you. I look forward to reconnecting with you from my new role at Office Y."

3) Do an exit interview with HR and, if appropriate, with the Big Boss.

4) Wipe your computer. Move important documents into a shared drive and gather anything useful onto a portable drive for your own future use. Delete everything else: your browser history, personal documents, and the contents of your inbox.

5) Stay until the end of the workday, then celebrate a job well done.

ACKNOWLEDGMENTS

Tremendous thanks go to Nick Fauchald and Dovetail Press, for blind trust, thoughtful collaboration, and treks to the Navy Yard; Marnie Hanel-Bordley, writer, fairy godmother, and accomplice, for her friendship; the inimitable Paul Bogaards, the toughest boss I've ever had—but also the most generous, and the best teacher; Michelle Ishay, for being a mentor and friend; Heather Halberstadt, for letting me through the VF doors; Aimee Bell, for steady wisdom and for showing me the path forward; TNY, floors 38 and 39; my cache of work sisters Annabelle, Allison, Carly, Cappi, Erica, JJ, Adrea, Nadine, Ella, and Dunia—I am honored to know you all; the Charlie Bird family; David Belt and Scott Cohen, for building New Lab and letting me be a part of it; Shirley, for changing everything; Stella, for teaching me more than I taught you; the Gold-Ermans, I love you; Grant, my love and the hardest-working person I've ever met; and The Worms, my longtime allies in figuring it out.

ABOUT THE AUTHOR

A writer and media strategist, Molly Erman is the director of communications for New Lab in the Brooklyn Navy Yard, a sprawling hub for advanced technology, including robotics, artificial intelligence, and connected devices. She cut her teeth in the New York publishing industry and is an alumna of *The New Yorker*, *Vanity Fair*, Artisan Books, and Alfred A. Knopf. Erman lives in Manhattan, where she strives to keep her houseplants alive.

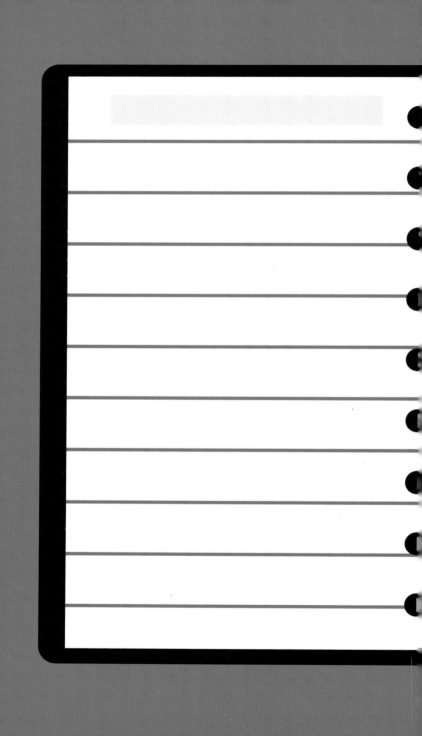

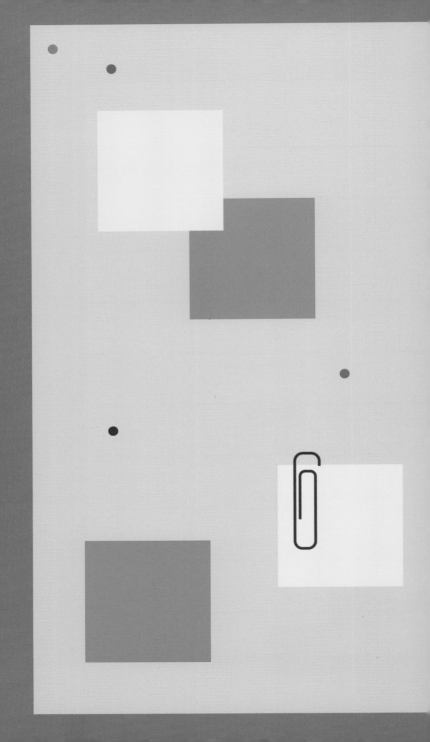

DOVETAIL

Published by Dovetail Press in Brooklyn, New York, a division of Assembly Brands LLC.

For details or ordering information, contact the publisher at the address below or email **info@dovetail.press**.

Dovetail Press
42 West Street #403
Brooklyn, NY 11222
www.dovetail.press

Library of Congress Cataloging-in-Publication data is on file with the publisher.

ISBN: 978-0-9898882-4-0

First Edition

Printed in the United States

10 9 8 7 6 5 4 3 2 1